LEAVING ATLANTIS

ACKNOWLEDGEMENTS

"Meeting-Point", "Finitude" and "Nursing Home" were first published in *Bim: Arts for the 21st Century*.

My gratitude to George Lamming who in various and complex ways inspired this collection. My special thanks to Edward Baugh, Keith Ellis, Kwame Dawes, Anthony Bogues and Hazel Simmons-McDonald for their critiques and ongoing encouragement. It has been a pleasure to share my poems with Robert Edison Sandiford, Linda Deane and other members of Writers Ink from whose valuable comments I have benefited.

I feel very fortunate to be among those Caribbean writers whose work is published by Peepal Tree Press. My heartfelt gratitude to editor and publisher, Jeremy Poynting. I also thank Hannah Bannister for her various skills including the artwork on the cover of the collection.

I appreciate the continuing support of Rixford and Barbara Mayers, Greta Prescott, Denese Nichols, Vivienne Roberts and my siblings Andy, Uriel, Althia, Judith. Henry and Sherrol. Special thanks to my mother, Clarene, and my daughter, Simone.

ESTHER PHILLIPS

LEAVING ATLANTIS

PEEPAL TREE

First published in Great Britain in 2015
Peepal Tree Press Ltd
17 King's Avenue
Leeds LS6 1QS
UK

ISBN: 9781845233143

Supported by
ARTS COUNCIL
ENGLAND

CONTENTS

To the Consummate Artist and my twin grandchildren,
Matthew Edward and Erin Louise.

COMING HOME

"The lord never send a bird
without a branch." — G.L's mother

So, love, light here,
now is your homing season.
There's a cry inside you still
that summoned revolution,
called forth the imagination:
the unconquerable domain.

Now, all across this archipelago
are those no longer daunted
by the world, no longer fearful
of dismantling one history
for another. Ancestral guardians
everywhere open the gates of memory
of origins we recognize at last as ours.

Lonely sea gull crying on the Atlantic,
you must not fear the folding of your wings.
It's your wide span over the Caribbean
and its diaspora we'll remember;
how you took the cruel burning,
casting what we feared was only
shadow, until our eyes could bear
the light of sovereignty you dreamt
for us and for our children.

So, love, light here.
Now is your homing season.
You have flown far.

NEXUS

You wear your need for me
like an affliction, some strange dis-
ease that overtook you unawares.
This need is your undoing,
this can't-wait-to-hear-her-voice-once-more
madness, your frenzy that would force
the hours to leap the two long days
since seeing her and seeing her again.

I am your loss of style:
the sad cessation of your old war-cry,
"Pursuer never, always pursued."
I am your dotage, your vulnerable
season. This need defies your old
philosophies, disputes your proven forms
of reasoning. You swear sometimes
I am your Nemesis, even.

I fear the day, my love,
when you should think this need
a burden that you cannot bear.

Be patient. Here is no sorcery,
no duplicitous entanglement.
The Hand that guided me to you
and you to me is stronger than my own.
A higher wisdom precontrives
the meeting of improbabilities.
So anxious need transformed
by love, may rest at ease.

MEETING-POINT

(for George & my grand-daughter, Zoe)

She had shed the "Uncle" at his bidding,
no doubt. "George," she calls,
sure of her place at the summit of the world,
"may I come in?" The door opens, a glimpse
of white hair, and she runs into the room.

We watch her transition from outright refusal
to, "My George". First the array of balloons
he bought and blew up himself, her three-year
old laughter artless, bursting free.
This playmate makes the funniest faces,
becomes her willing audience as she reads the stories
she contrives; she sings for him, she dances.

We watch him reading silently. She, eyeing him
all the while, waits with the rarest patience.
Perhaps this book will teach him how to answer
all the "Whys?" she's heaping up,
or prompt him to another round of games.

Time, too, is playing its peculiar game:
old age recedes, philosophy declines, all titles bow.
Inside this room he is a child again, and she,
unwise as yet to his burden of years, lifts
it as lightly as the ball they toss between them,
or the yellow balloon floating outside the room.

YOU ANOTHER COUNTRY

You are yourself another country;
your own prime meridian.
"It's easy," you said, " here's the key."
So I took courage and entered
thick forests, borders, pathways turning
and turning on themselves.
I tried to track you where your light
seemed brightest: your monument of thought.
Meteors clashed there, time shifted. Black holes
spewed out destinies of a New World.

I searched for calmer spaces.
Somewhere inside these tangled forests
there must be a tract where sunlight falls,
soft rain nurtures green shoots, and the sound
of the wind as it rises is the call of a heart –

Not every journey ends at Heartease.
Another mettle forges some pathways:
an axis underlies each turning
and friction lends its radiance
to the shadowy places. The seeker learns
to shape her own heart's harbour.

But you are not all forest.
You're unexpected springs where lines
still intersect. And all along your landscape,
meteor trails lay claim to the imagination,
that sovereign state where kindred souls thrive best –
You are a country worthy of habitation.

TRANSITION RADIO

*(on breaking the news that someone had stolen his German-
made Grundig radio while in my keeping)*

Don't get vex, love,
is you who praise Caliban
fuh tiefin words from European.
Talk 'bout battle fuh language!
Talk 'bout struggle!
You should see how small de space is
he come through! He tek out louvres,
scale a wall – a historic mission.

So yes, he tief de Grundig radio
dat you used to own,
but think 'bout all de language
now in Caliban possession:
all dat learned discourse
on global upheaval
de BBC world news,
de latest Book Reviews –

*Pardon me? By now the thief must have sold
the damned radio for just a few dollars!*

Well… ahm… when it comes to language,
ain't you the one who see continuing
possibility? Caliban just expanding
his options. Is cultural emancipation,
love, is culture in transition.

UNSEEN

Often there
in your river-surge
of voice
like silt, like debris
diverging
through twisted roots;
I heard them
when in your deep-
throated discourse
you debated them,
sometimes with loud
passion
or in a mere whisper.
I saw them
in your careful scrutiny
of my face, the sudden
shifting of your eyes,
a quick smile hidden,
not to be shared.

They were sent to bind
your heart, your tongue.
Cleft-handed,
they loosed your brain
only for seasons.

But I know them now.
I do not fear them.
I am my grand-
mother's child
and she was
a demon-fighting woman.
I heard her cry out
on her knees.

I saw her tarry
on mission hall floors,
lips cracked from fasting,
until one day
a wing-rush,
Heaven open,
hex gone –
and look how
river flow free
with a clear shining.

PAPER TRAILING

(for George on his 80th birthday)

I'd thought that for all
your sorting, tearing,
putting aside,
you were content
in your *stable*.
You and paper
have held each other
hostage for decades
on end – a familiar torment –

until belly sickened
with words,
you'd let the page
have it! Green, black,
yellow bile forging,
reshaping islands,
sinking empire;
and in the terror of the moment,
the page yielded, multiplied.

I'm not so sure
what this putting aside,
sorting, tearing might mean now –
Clearing out?

AND YET AGAIN

Tonight I want to offer you
this moonlight cupped in a purple
flower, this chorus of crickets
holding no grudge against the day's
dying. I want to lift the cool sweetness
of sour-grass under the night wind
and soothe the tautness in your face.
I want to tempt you away from your heroic
silence for joy that is free and foolish.
I want to weave these early stars
like a rope for you to hold
and make your way past your old
hurts, faiths crumbling like dust.
This wanting is not a nebulous thing;
it is the soul desiring its other self
where need knows no hindrance of words.

Now, only this longing, this reaching
yet again – in spite of.

ARRIVAL

Why now, why now this
evening time when, as you say,
your flag is flying at half-mast?
And Captain, O my Captain,
what is this cargo that you bring me?
Stones of sapphire turning to stars
between your fingers? Rubies
gleaned where the river bends
at Belle Vue, Sans Souci?

Such was the bounty you brought
another love, who counted with leaves,
tender and green from the woods
in spring, your vows of homecoming.
I could have told her,
oh, I could have told her, leaves
wither and glass houses splinter.

I too have gathered
stones on a faraway shore
where the hurricane's eye,
swollen, slept for a moment,
and I gathered stones to mark my praise.

And shall I tell you?
Will you believe me when I tell you
that on that day I dreamt I found the pebble
you had hidden under the grape-leaf,
I saw it changed, crystallized
into word and into meaning?

If you would know this meaning,
come with me, not far along this shore
where grape trees cut a path

by the sandbank. There you will
hear a voice ancient with knowing
that a man, weary from seeking,
may find at last what he once sought
in the arms of lovers,
in the wide ocean's heart,
in the pride of reason:

a pebble changed into a pearl.

And for this Pearl he trades
his other kingdoms.

NIGHT ERRANT

You hate the ignoble
thing, the unworthy.
You believe man is
the measure (despite
your brilliance.)
So when the wolf
rips the night open –
the night you had so drawn
with soft colours –
you deny, you deny,
you deny.
And the creature
on cue, disappears.
The air, snarled, lies
heavy between us.

I've not much use
for a cerebral-shaped heart
nurtured on some one-eyed
philosophy.

Love me with your own
heart hoarding the traitor,
the rough rage, your un-
certain compassion.

EXIT I

The arc fragments.
The swift detour
confounds a journey.

You who delighted
in impermanence
called Atlantis *home*.
Perhaps it was the disorder
you needed: rusty iron
bannisters, cracked,
drooping ceilings,
plaster peeling off walls,
doors heavy with salt air
resisting closure;
everything moving
towards some possibility
fluid as the sea.

You and the ebb
and flow were one;
each coming and going –
no questions asked –
just the leaving
and the arriving.

In the sea's permanence,
no two waves are the same:
one breaks
before the other
unfolds itself.

EXIT II

To pack an old man's life
into cardboard boxes,
while plaster falls from cracked
ceilings, salt-rusted hinges
no longer fasten the doors,
and a single wood-dove
calls in the distance,
is not an easy thing.

That builders have come
with unkind haste to gauge
the length and height of new walls,
while the old man's hustling
his memories out of corners
and floorboards (his allies
of long years). This is not right.

All morning the blue van
comes and goes, fetching
more and more boxes
as if to say, "This is it.
All ends here."

By evening the white-haired man
sits in the car following behind
while the van makes its final
journey back up the hill.

But from the bent of his shoulders
and the grief in his eyes,
he remains at Atlantis still.

BIRTHDAY VISIT TO CUBA

How the skies spoke on your birthday!
the same reverberation I've heard
in your voice – only this morning
there's an ellipsis in the echo.

For these ten days you're harvest-
ing memories I cannot share.
You are bone-gathering:
a fist once folded in defiance,
the feet that spurned an empire
hobbled now among gravestones;
a headband red as Rodney's blood
bleached by the years' indifference.

They fete you, as they rightly should.
While the young and bright pay tribute
to title and tenure, you sit, half-listening,
honing your reluctant peace.

You see how the *Beast* may win after all:
its subterranean smell invades the city
in the half smirk on the cashier's face;
the branding of appetite with cell phones
and DVD players; the brag of steel
and chrome over iron, cracked but enduring,
a barter of nation for illusion of capital.

When you return, I'll have a meal,
a change of clothing, a space for luggage
ready for you. But there's not room enough
to house the ashes your eyes may speak of.

HE LISTENS

Searching his eyes, I venture only
his small frailties at first. He smiles.
Encouraged, I press on. (He's sensitive.
No doubting that ever again!)
This time he does not say that these are mere
formalities (what "these" does he mean?
My woes are not a matter of propriety!)

I question in more ways than one his failure
to connect with me when I most need him to.
My remonstrations do not make him flinch.
(What stoicism! None of the jitters
or impatience of a younger man.)

But shouldn't he respond to me by now?
I ask him (word-master that he is) could he
have missed the meaning of my simple language?

Surely that's not a smile he's holding back!
Surely he knows I'm serious!
But no, his gaze is steady on my face, and
for the next ten minutes, he's listening.

At last I sink, grateful, though spent,
into his arms and spy, under a pamphlet lying near,
his hearing-aid he'd placed discreetly on the chair.

AIR

It's how the air enters a room
lingers in breath, sweat,
perfume; draws out from walls
the drift of voices,
transmutes into a hum
the turbulence under civil
words or shelters some pre-
vailing grief in quiet corners.

If only the pulsing air
its throb and quiver of joy
would so remain; ignite the
eye and heart

as does the hummingbird who
every day lights up
the old fence in iridescent
greens and blues,
sucks sweet nectar
from morning-glory

then hovers
shuttle-dancer
wing-whistler
resounding the air.

NEAR DISTANCE

At last the heart makes its way
past sadness, regret,
grows at ease with shadows
that move like humble servants
about the room,
sweeping up words
where they had fallen
as dust motes, unconnected
from anything we meant to say;

brushing the edge off memory,
turning it face downwards,
tending its slow seepage
into the daily habit
of absence
under one roof.

MESSENGER

When evening
after evening
your anger
wordless
unassailable
stalks the corridor,
wafts its odour
through every room
from floor to ceiling,

I find myself listening
for your real footfall
softer
softer
almost limping
into this second
shifting light.

Where is your voice,
that beam that cut
the ear and eye
of Antillean indifference?
No more?

This sound in the silence
still surprises me:
Triton's heart breaking,
his conch-shell laid aside
dusk-gathering.

COURAGE

This night, while cricket-
song throbs in my veins
like glad cymbals,
and the frog's whistle,
the wind's sway
and the beating pulse are one;
tonight while fireflies
disarm the darkness,
I can venture out
to where you are.

I carry within me the lamp
burning at the kitchen-table;
the gaslight hovering over the old
people's hymns packed with hope.

This armour fits well and will not rub
against my chafing heart. A brew
of flower-fence and fit-weed calms me.

Tonight, with my mother's honest
rawness at my back, her calling

a spade nothing but what it was,
I can run my finger along your contra-
dictions and not flinch.

IN-SIGHT

This morning, the silence
shakes its old armour off,
makes room for the drift of voices:
Can't you see? Can't you see?
And I do, after all this time.

I see how you brought me
this huge bowl of trust
and I caught it,
so used to the weight of others.

Did I let you down?
Not in my faithfulness
that is inviolate,
nor in some battery of words,

but in the web, the grain,
the fine shading of you?

Was I dreaming
when you took your trust back?
Yet, give me one thread
and I'll find you again
in this dawning.

MORNING

Is this the morning
I may be tender with you;
put away the coldness
I clasp as a shield?

You see how easily
I touch the white flower,
the bright sage.
Must I bind my hands
when I'm near you?

Is this the morning
I may be quiet with you;
feel the old ease between us
when we had no need
for measuring our words?

Perhaps I'll walk into the room,
place my hand on your shoulder,
let it linger for a while;
see that old familiar gesture
when you move your hand across
your cheek as if to wipe away
a shy, reluctant smile.

Then, your hand over mine,
we'll look to see how a long
and obdurate night may yield,
give way to the memory
of other mornings
tender as this.

DISTILLATION

I put the drops
into his eyes
on mornings
and
at night

With every
drop

I pray
for
light

PATRIARCHY

That night at the dinner-table, a familiar tension
hugged the air: your old war against *corporate
middle-class barbarism*.
You were battling against your hosts' *compliance*,
your voice a canon in full resonance,
and in those moments you were my father,
though his was a more direct engagement with Lucifer.

I might have read the clues: the same small room
crammed with books on every wall, across the floor,
clutter where every breathing space should be;
blood-ties held loosely like rags;
a sharp eye out for the innocent acolyte.

"FEELING"

The word in his mouth
is prodigal, recalcitrant, erring.
He cannot persuade the word
to render its meaning.
Feeling is like a fugitive
who holds some memory
of home but cannot close
the distance, an outcast
looking to the joys
of others, but obdurate
in his self-inflicted exile.

Feeling just yielded up its power
to stronger foes: Disinclination,
Lack of Intention.

Who knows when Feeling
trailed its way up to Mt. Misery
and like the Tribe Boys
leaned its head over the edge
and said farewell.

STONE WALL

Near every line a Lazarus lurks.
His breath stirs the air.
Across the page his shadow,
like parched leaves, falls
for a long moment.

His stench fills the room.
You open the window
but never enough,
lest you forget your own
downward journey

that says you must create,
though your eyes and hands
are bound.
You wait for the word
to unwrap its layers
so only the core remains.

Your three days
are three thousand years.

Until a voice says, "Come."
Weightless as air
you rise upward
from the unhewn rock
to meet the Word
where Art gives in
at last
to meaning.

THE LADY AND THE JAR

After he left she crawled
inside the crystal jar, inhabiting
his absence among the leaves
she counted until his return:

three hundred and fifty days of miles
one thousand and one days
one thousand and eleven miles of days
one hundred and eighty days –

Hers was a whole forest she could
throw to the wind; fill the air
with auguries of her freedom,
should she so choose.

True, she smashed the crystal jars
she'd stored on her shelves,
but could not crush the viscid jar
she'd grown inside herself:

repository of jewels
smeared with the slime
of Demon coast;
pearls that were
the murdered eyes
of children,
bones of Tribes-
women who mined
the soil with naked hands
in sorrow
for their murdered men.

Better dead leaves of endless days
than the blood of conquest

staining her jar,
when the moon hid for shame
and the cloud refused its covering.

SAD OFFICERS

(after Thom Gunn's "My Sad Captains")

Three shadows appear on the deck
in the moonlight: officers and
therefore "men on the inside".
How late they learn the lessons
of a future they refused!
But before they leave, they stand

transparent, at last, in the unyielding glow,
their past encircling them like a girdle of infamy.
They were men who, it seemed, lived only
to exact the right of gold and glory;
the might that past and future would applaud.

They are not at rest.
They witness their moments of glory
made of little account. And turning away from
the redeeming San Cristobal, past pride or ire,
they walk into the dark, emblazoned
in the night's white arc of fire.

TURNING

All crossroads are guarded by angels

An ageing man stands in the twilight,
dazed, his tomes lying beside him.
He retraces his steps along a path
he thought he knew,
finds it unfamiliar, consults
the signposts, picks up his tomes
again, leafs through them slowly.

Surely the ancient heads knew
what they were talking about:
the existential angst assuaged
by duty ending in Nothing;
the social man buttressed by learning,
all gods banished from the universe.

But, O, his need! His need!

Only one glimmering Book remains.
It is to this path, while the dark
tide rises, that he turns.

PEBBLE. CRAB. IRON

Unseeing, as the crab's dead eye,
you seek the pebble under a pile
of withering leaves;
a pebble that has survived
attenuation
attrition
dislocation.

Lest you profane it with your touch
or taint its smooth complexion,
bright in the ring of shadow,

consider this fragment
of unhewn stone
broken from some altar;
a token of sacrifice
atonement
a triumph over trial
and sorrow.

You can no more contain
this pebble than the hand
can seize the wind.
Seek only its meaning:
the dead crab disintegrates,
the unstable iron falls to rust.
But the pebble you see
then do not see,
it is the enduring spirit
that lives as well on earth
wind and water —
and cannot die.

RIVAL

He came to me, early, with the scent
of carnations, anthurium lilies
and the heat rising off the tar-
road in the afternoon sun.

How could a child's singing draw him?
Yet he came to my grandmother's front-
house as I sat alone and the old Sankey
drew song after song from me.

There he was, his breath rustling
the yellow lace curtains, feet tapping,
keeping time with the grandfather clock
above the mahogany cabinet, his hand
soft as feathers on my head.

When it rained and thunder almost
cracked the roof open, "Master,
the tempest is raging," I sang anxiously.
His answer, "Child, be still. Be at peace.
I love you and my love will never cease."
And though I cannot tell exactly how,
he captured my heart.

Now you call him rival: joy-stealer,
beguiler, myth-maker.
And yet, how strange a rival
who would so compel the one He loves
to love the one that so opposes Him.

NIGHT OF THE ALBA

The audience sees you standing
behind the podium, but I know
you've long flattened the walls
of the room; you've gone leaping
across the Caribbean Sea.

There you spin and toss the islands.
Like a fuller's earth you filter out
the slag of insularity, the waste
of creeping nationalism
until one shining stretch remains –
one place with one foundation,
one home named Region.

The crowd's applause signals your return.
O Captain, your sea-legs are weary;
you make your way towards me,
grasp with both of yours, the hand
I'm holding out.

You're anchored.

REVOLUTION

How to revolve harmoniously
around a fixed point has always
been our question.
You, with your Marxist stance.
Me, with my love of Christ.

You waged a patient war against
my "closed" mind. Book after book
informed me how a Marxist looked
at Jesus; symbolism, not the literal,
was the enlightened approach;
the Word was mired in politics and fable.

Again, how to resolve the question
of the body? For you, the seat of pleasure.
For me, however sweet its plunder,
still the temple.

Product of history and social formation –
the sum total, in your view, of the human.
I hold man is his dual nature:
God-shaped though flawed and prone to error.

*   *   *

How are we now, years on
from earlier tensions when we thought it
worth our while to strive for common ground?

I've opened the door much wider
to your deity, Reason, but find him shy
of going beyond my mind.
I've asked him what is this essential
loneliness? Why seek purpose and

meaning? Why long for certainty
and what is the source of that longing?

Why poetry? From what abyss
does poetry spring – distilled, clearer
than thought, multi-hued, each sense held
in abeyance to its wonder?

How does Faith cast her upward beam
and reconfigure stars?

But more than all, Reason remains
dumbfounded when I ask him this:
what is that greater Love
that makes me love you still?

GLEANING

Why should this harvest
of your evening years be mine?
Where was I in your wild,
wild rain?
What rock sheltered me
until the fury passed?

Yet in these tranquil times –
I long for tempest.

FINITUDE

He is the kite-flyer, whose upward gaze
forgets the finite ball of twine that spirals
out until the hand is empty.

The man who from a distance celebrates Nothing,
only to find the closer he gets, that nothing can exist
outside of something: desire, pleasure, pain.
It was always not possible to choose only Nothing.

He daily flogs the mind that must not yield
to Time's nudges; its kick in the ribs,
the years' shuffling one truth after another.

How faithfully he tends the body's needs
yet longs for its annihilation.

His conversations are with the dead.
His voice is the echo of bones.
The pages crumble in his careful hands

WILL

I place the single sheet of paper
inside my drawer.
Your words I cannot shut away:
my death, my burial, my mother's grave.
This weight of absence I must bear.

Did you think, love, that these
were mere instructions I should follow?
What you've handed me is one empty
morning after another, no sound

of your slippers shuffling down
the corridor, the peculiar creak
of your bedroom door, your keys
striking the gate as you collect
the morning paper.

I've seen what you call the body's
betrayal: the slowing steps, loss
of hearing, a voice that once
made mischief with the heart
barely resonant now.

Though I'm one for the quiet tide,
aftermath, dry season. It is this yielding,
this final folding I can't get used to.

NURSING HOME

There'll be no greater light.
It's dim, as it should be.
All is grim here.
(G.L)

See how they've draped death
across that chair,
limbs hanging loosely,
skin fresh as a newborn
except for the stillness;
the gaze, it seems,
sucked into the white wall.

Silence quells the unexpected word,
the odd chuckle. Only the night
finds credence here: the painful cries,
an anguish of unspoken loneliness.

Philosopher, your chair now sits
on wheels, guided by a kind nurse.
How can you bear to witness the fall
of reason, when the mind gives way,
what is real trumps the imagination,
and language knows no skill
to counter the void?

You speak of giving your books away
as if to shed some weight.
 It is the season for light travelling
when all, *all* is left at the Gate.

NO WAITING HERE

For goodness sake,
don't be like the Rilke character
who makes a vocation of waiting –
especially for death!

Why pay death such homage?
Why fold each day away,
eyes averted
but with such patient care,
as if it were a gift
you were offering up?

The days are already Death's domain.
He stakes them out. He marks them
with his inexpungible pen.
He's at the end of the long, last
wailing cry; the peaceful sigh.
He comes whether we wait or not.

When he comes to this room,
as he will some day, let him enter,
not with his territorial tread, but edge-
wise, shading his eyes at the light
you've let into the room.

Let him touch your eyelids, timidly,
abashed at the life held firm in your gaze,
a harvest of thought his claim can't erase;
the memory of days you carved out by fire,
defying an empire in the face of old laws.

In the end Death won't wait.
Yet you may give *him* pause.

A PRECIPITATE SORROW

I live too much in the now, the flame,
the thunder of you. When you are gone,
how often will I turn an evening's silence
into a rosary, coaxing the past with crystal
beads, if only… if only…
How will I unhear, untouch memory?
How dilute your gaze, remove
its essence like the years' varnish,
from all we loved?

Perhaps the mystery dimmed now
by the familiar will come again,
and distance (the endless exile!)
will draw you closer beyond
the feel of flesh.

After months have passed,
when it's only the wind and my fingers
turning the pages, I'll read your
conversations of age and innocence again.

No longer your bright shadow
over my shoulder, the lucent filter
of your mind to clarify, expand.
Yet every message, each edict
amplified by absence.

I'm told I should ask all the questions
now, record word and gesture,
nuance and circumstance,
as if Time were mine to mediate,
devise moment with meaning, arrange
or label for future conveyers of history.

And yet, I negotiate – make a dry-run
of tomorrow's grief against the long, slow
hours when I shall wish my heart a palimpsest.

ACCEPTANCE

From where I stand in the kitchen, I see
your white hair slowly ascending the stairs,
and wonder if the nights are still unkind;
what demons are waiting as you cross
the landing and how you combat them with
your failing strength. Does your old weapon
of reason still come to your rescue
or has time rusted its edge?

These walls are now our mediation;
our buffer against the contagion
of words; our final surrender
to a distance we cannot close.

Such strange peace.

NOTES

p. 9: "Lonely sea gull crying on the Atlantic" references a line from Eric Roach's poem, "Letter to Lamming", *The Flowering Rock: Collected Poems 1938-1974* (Leeds: Peepal Tree Press, 1992, 2012), p. 81.

p. 12: The journey to "Heartease" references Lorna Goodison's collection of that name – (London, New Beacon Books, 1988).

p. 18: "I dreamt I found the pebble/you had hidden" references the pebble hidden by the boy, G, in *The Castle of My Skin* (1953)

p. 21, 22: "Atlantis" – refers to the Atlantis Hotel, Bathsheba, George Lamming's home for many years, which he had to leave with very little warning from the new owners.

p. 32: "Engagement with Lucifer" – my father is a minister of religion.

p. 33: "Tribeboys" – this references the native figures in the legend told by the little Society of the four boys in George Lamming's *Of Age and Innocence* (1958). In the legend, rather than submit to the invader Bandit Kings, the Tribeboys climb to the top of Mount Misery and "dive to their own funeral". (Leeds, Peepal Tree Press, Caribbean Modern Classics Edition, 2011), p. 121.

p. 35: "The Lady and the Jar" references the Lady of the Black Rock from Lamming's *Natives of My Person* (1972).

p. 37: "three shadows" references seafaring characters in Lamming's novel *Natives of My Person* (1972). San Cristobal is Lamming's imaginary, composite Caribbean island, the location of several of his novels.

p. 39: "Pebble. Crab. Iron." – this references the episode in *Of Age and Innocence* when the returning intellectual, Mark Kennedy, comes to a realisation of the depth of his alienation as he sits on a beach observing "a pebble, a piece of iron and a dead crab" (Peepal Tree Press Modern Classics Edition, p. 94).

p. 40: "Sankey" – Hymnal of sacred songs written by Ira. D. Sankey during the nineteenth century.

p. 41: "Night of the Alba". George Lamming was awarded the 2011 Alba Award of Letters at UWI, Cave Hill.

ABOUT THE AUTHOR

Esther Phillips won a James Michener fellowship to the University of Miami where she gained an MFA degree in Creative Writing, 1999. She won the Alfred Boas Poetry Prize of the Academy of American Poets for her poetry collection/thesis and went on to win the Frank Collymore Literary Endowment Award in 2001. Her publications are: Chapbook, *La Montee* (UWI, 1983); *When Ground Doves Fly* (Ian Randle Publishers, Kingston, 2003); *The Stone Gatherer* (Peepal Tree Press, 2009.) Esther Phillips represented Barbados at the Poetry Parnassus Festival in London, 2012 and her poem "Word" was selected by BBC Scotland to represent her country at the 2014 Commonwealth Games. She has read her work at various literary festivals, including Calabash, in 2009 and her poems appear in several anthologies, including *Poetas de caribe anglophono* (Casa de las Americas, 2011) and *Give the Ball to the Poet* (Cambridge-Homerton, 2014)). Esther Phillips is editor of *Bim: Arts for the 21st Century* and is founder of Writers Ink Inc., as well as the Bim Literary Festival & Book Fair. In 2014, Esther Phillips' poetry was recorded for the Poetry Archive, U.K. She was born and lives in Barbados.

ALSO BY ESTHER PHILLIPS

The Stone Gatherer
ISBN: 9781845230852; pp. 64; pub. 2009; price £7.99

There is a candour to Esther Phillips's affecting collection of poems, *The Stone Gatherer*, that can be quite disarming. In poems that undress the foibles of family – a father's masks and a mother's "fortissimo" – there is tenderness and affection despite the pain. Here is a poet's voice that seeks and finds grace notes in the spaces between experience. Hers is a poetics that locates itself in the landscape of Barbados, displaying a facility for the Barbadian dialect and the lyrical West Indian English of the major poets that have come before her. The collection's structure is a woman-centred movement of poems that begins with the complex coming-of-age journey of a child, through an adulthood of romance and crushed emotions, through the rewards and anxieties of motherhood, to the contemplative and reflective place of maturity where a woman assumes the role of elder, protector of the community, and of prophet. Phillips embraces all of these roles in her poems, allowing us to enjoy what becomes an expansive narrative through time and life's changes. She shows herself to have the wit and intelligence of an artist committed to the use of verse to test the meaning of experience. And yet in all of this, we are often most struck by Phillips's eye for detail, her sense of landscape and her willingness to locate her poems in the world that moves and breathes around her.

In *The Stone Gatherer*, one has the sense of an artist collecting stones of different shapes and dimensions, arranging them in such a way that there is space enough for them to breathe and for us to pause to think and feel.